Touch of
Silk

Touch of Silk

CRESCENT BOOKS

It is believed that the first recorded undergarment appears on a Greek fresco in Sicily. The scene depicts a woman with bound breasts but on closer inspection one realises that she is an athlete. Necessity, ever the Mother of Invention, had created the bandeau top which is still with us today and never more so than in the 1980s when many of the new bikinis and one piece bathing suits reflect the style of that Grecian athlete.

The need for lingerie in its various forms has always been dictated by the fashions and styles of the times and by women wanting to change their natural shapes to fit these styles. Perhaps the greatest changes took place in the late 18th century when, following the French Revolution and the preceding period of hooped petticoats and corseted figures, the new Directoire style was born. This return to the classical style of late Greek and Roman costume indicated a more liberated and natural line. Corsets disappeared and the waist line moved up to just under the breasts. In the early part of the 19th century enthusiasm for the classical style became a passion which reached its climax during the Napoleonic Empire. Skirts were raised to the ankle and suddenly the pantalet, the forerunner of the bikini brief, emerged frilled, lacy and beguiling.

Over the next hundred years corsets returned with a vengeance but it was not until after the First World War that lingerie, as we know it today, first appeared. The newly liberated and emancipated woman of the 1920s rejected the feminine shape, skirts rose even higher and suddenly bust bodices, bust depressers and functional undergarments had arrived. Previously lingerie had always been made of cotton but now French knickers, camisoles and cami-knickers were produced in crêpe-de-Chine, silks, satins and laces very similar to those that have re-appeared in the last ten years.

The last and greatest innovation of the 20th century was the bra which finally emerged, cantilevered and engineer-designed to 'support and project' Jane Russell's bust for a film in the late 40s. The bosom has never looked back although the bra has changed, as fashion dictated, and was even abandoned altogether for a while in the 60s!

Today lingerie is both simple and functional, luxurious and impractical. The specialist lingerie stores reckon that men represent thirty percent of their customers, buying maybe three times a year for anniversaries or special occasions. They seem to know what they want and it is usually sexy! In the last ten years, garter belts, with matching bra and briefs have been hot favourites, closely followed by cami-knickers and French knickers in silks and satins with even the odd diamond or two carefully stitched into the embroidery.

Perhaps the biggest single influence on lingerie today is the fact that it is bought to be seen. In the words of the song:
"In olden days a glimpse of stocking
Was looked on as something shocking
Now heaven knows!
Anything goes!

She's beautiful and therefore to be woo'd;
She is a woman, therefore to be won.

William Shakespeare

Women are like tricks by slight of hand,
Which, to admire, we should not understand.

William Congreve

I have heard with admiring submission
the experience of the lady who declared
that the sense of being well-dressed
gives a feeling of inward tranquility
which religion is powerless to bestow.

Ralph Waldo Emerson

Fie, fie upon her!
There's language in her eye, her cheek,
    her lip,
Nay, her foot speaks; her wanton spirits
    look out
At every joint and motive of her body.

William Shakespeare

Lovely forms do flow
From conceit divinely framed;
Heaven is music, and thy beauty's
Birth is heavenly.

Thomas Campion

Women are much more like each other than men:
they have, in truth, but two passions, vanity and
love; these are their universal characteristics.

The Earl of Chesterfield

A daughter of gods, divinely tall
And most divinely fair.

Alfred, Lord Tennyson

If I could write the beauty of your eyes
And in fresh numbers all your graces,
The age to come would say, "This poet lies;
Such heavenly touches ne'er touched earthly faces."

William Shakespeare

My mother bids me bind my hair
With bands of rosy hue,
Tie up my sleeves with ribbons rare,
And lace my bodice blue.

Anne Hunter

She is Venus when she smiles;
But she's Juno when she walks,
And Minerva when she talks.

Ben Jonson

Whenas in silks my Julia goes
Then, (methinks) how sweetly
    flows
That liquefaction of her clothes.

Robert Herrick

She just wore
Enough for modesty – no more.

Robert Williams Buchanan

I'll come no more
behind your scenes, David;
for the silk stockings
and white bosoms of your actresses
excite my amorous propensities.

Samuel Johnson

Give me a look, give me a face
That makes simplicity a grace;
Robes loosely flowing, hair as free:
Such sweet neglect more taketh me.

Ben Jonson

She knows her man, and when you rant and swear
Can draw you to her *with a single hair.*

John Dryden

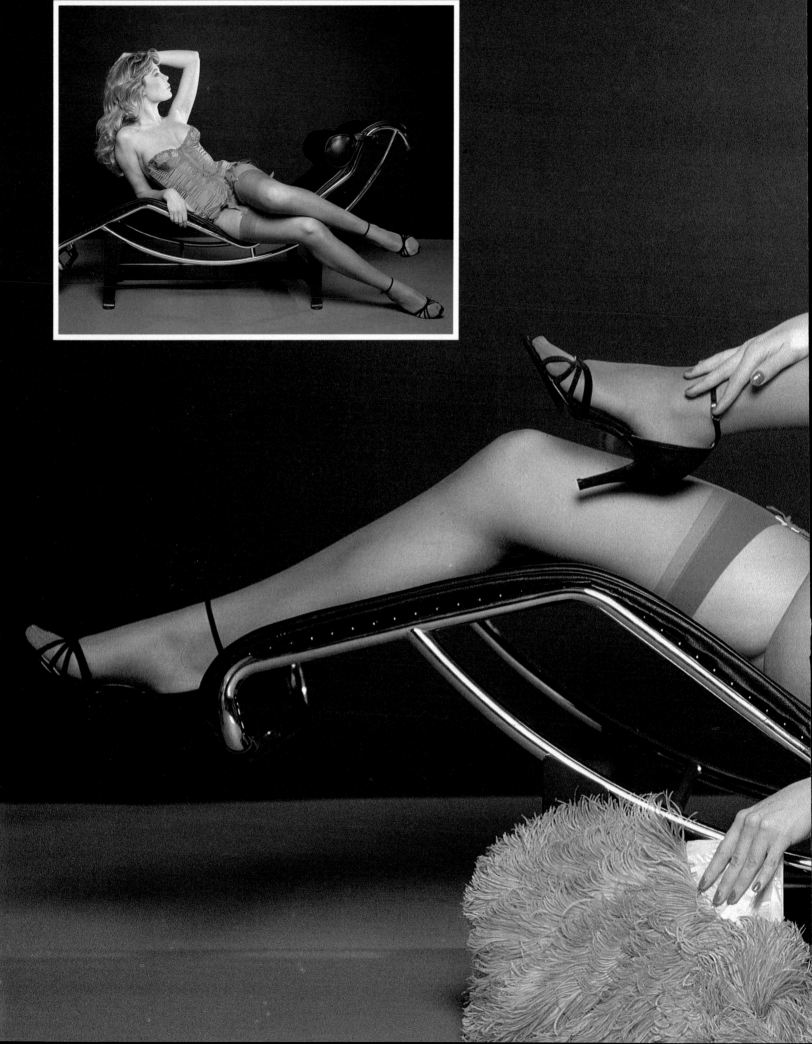

A sweet disorder in the dress
Kindles in clothes a wantonness:

Robert Herrick

From women's eyes this doctrine I derive:
They sparkle still the right Promethean fire;
They are the books, the arts, the academes,
That show, contain and nourish all the world.

William Shakespeare

What is your sex's earliest, latest care,
Your heart's supreme ambition? – To be fair.

George, Lord Lyttelton

And as she look'd about, she did
    behold,
How over that same door was
    likewise writ,
Be bold, be bold, and everywhere
    Be bold.

Edmund Spenser

I expect that Woman
will be the last thing
civilised by Man.

George Meredith

Careless she is with artful care,
Affecting to seem unaffected.

William Congreve

I for one venerate a petticoat.

Lord Byron

Cruelty has a human heart,
And Jealousy a human face;
Terror the human form divine,
and Secrecy the human dress.

William Blake

She was a phantom of delight
When first she gleaned upon my sight;
A lovely apparition sent
To be a moment's ornament;

William Wordsworth

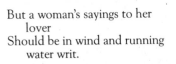

But a woman's sayings to her
   lover
Should be in wind and running
   water writ.

Catullus

I must have women.
There is nothing unbends the mind like them.

John Gay

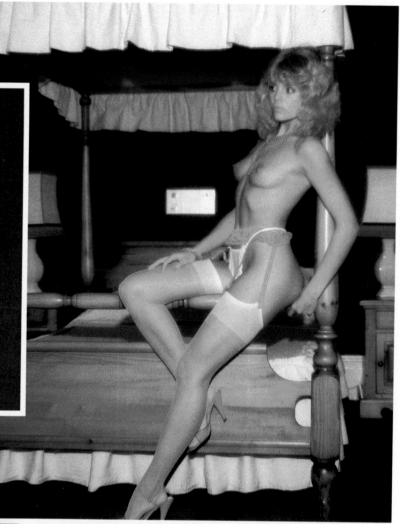

If the heart of a man is deprest with cares,
The mist is dispell'd when a woman appears.

John Gay

Sabrina fair,
Listen where thou art sitting
Under the glassy, cool,
        translucent wave,
In twisted braids of lilies knitting
The loose train of thy amber-
        dropping hair.

John Milton